KU-251-979

TURRIFF ACADEMY
LIBRARY

361.7

OXFAM

ELSPETH CLAYTON
(SERIES EDITOR: ROB ALCRAFT)

First published in Great Britain by Heinemann Library
Halley Court, Jordan Hill, Oxford OX2 8EJ
a division of Reed Educational and Professional Publishing Ltd

OXFORD FLORENCE PRAGUE MADRID ATHENS
MELBOURNE AUCKLAND KUALA LUMPUR SINGAPORE TOKYO
IBADAN NAIROBI KAMPALA JOHANNESBURG GABORONE
PORTSMOUTH NH CHICAGO MEXICO CITY SAO PAULO

Produced by Plum Creative (01590 612970)
Printed in China

01 00 99 98 97
10 9 8 7 6 5 4 3 2 1

ISBN 0 431 02746 3

British Library Cataloguing in Publication Data
    Clayton, Elspeth
    Oxfam. - (Taking Action)
    1. Shelter - Juvenile literature
    361.7'632'0941

Acknowledgements
The publishers would like to thank the following for permission to reproduce photographs.
Shafiqul Alam 12, 13; Shahidul Alam 7; Adrian Arbib 12, 13, 19; Badal 5; Brian Beardwood 22; Daniel Berinson 14, 15, 29; Keith Bernstein 29; E Clayton 4; Howard Davies 18, 19; Robert Davies 21; Nic Dunlop 26, 27, 29; Nancy Durrell-McKenna 4; Julio Etchart 7, 8; Mike Goldwater 6; Ana-Cecilia Gonzalez 23, 28; Jeremy Hartley 8, 9; James Hawkins 24; Crispin Hughes 6, 9, 10, 11, 20, 21; Joe Human 7; Rob Judges 25; Jenny Matthews 28, 29; Geoff Sayer 16, 17, 25; Sean Sprague 28.

Cover illustration by Scott Rhodes.

Every effort has been made to contact copyright holders of any material reproduced in this book. Any omissions will be rectified in subsequent printings if notice is given to the publisher.

All words in the text appearing in bold like **this** are explained in the Glossary.

CONTENTS

WHAT'S THE PROBLEM?

The problem is poverty. Poverty can mean a lot of different things. Being poor can mean not having enough to eat – not just for an hour or two, or a day or two, but for months, or even years. Imagine never being able to eat enough food to stop feeling hungry.

Poverty can mean never having enough money to be able to pay for all the things you need: clothes, somewhere to live, or medicine when you're ill.

Or it can mean having just enough money to survive but no more; having no money in case of an emergency, and no money to do the things you'd like to. It can mean thinking you'll never be able to make life better.

▼ **Baba Ismail, who lives in Pakistan, knows all about being poor: 'We are caught in the grip of poverty. We are struggling hard, but nothing changes.'**

There are more poor people in the world today than 50 years ago.

WHO IS POOR?

Often, particular groups are poor because they are overlooked, and need help to be noticed even by their communities. All over the world, groups such as racial minorities, old people, children and women often do not have a real say in the decisions that affect them.

Jamal's family lives in one of the **bustees** (slums) on the edge of Dhaka, in Bangladesh. Jamal says: 'Every day we look for work. If we don't get work, we don't get paid or eat.

When we get work, we work the whole day. We have no time to enjoy ourselves. We sleep as soon as we have eaten.'

This is what life is like for millions of families around the world. They work all day, every day, just to earn enough to survive.

These are the kinds of people Oxfam works with.

Jamal's family's land was washed away by a flood. With nowhere to live or to grow food, they moved to the city to look for work. Now they live here in one of Dhaka's *bustees*.

The world's poorest 50 countries are home to 80% of the world's people.

WHAT DOES OXFAM DO?

Oxfam began in 1942, during World War II. In towns all over the UK, groups of people collected parcels of food and clothes to send to families whose lives had been destroyed by the war. Oxfam was a group started in Oxford. Many of the groups stopped when the war ended, but Oxfam carried on – there were still millions of families needing help. Oxfam has been helping people whose lives have been torn apart by war and violence ever since.

There hasn't been a single day without a war somewhere in the world since 1942. Oxfam is helping people to make improvements in their communities, and helping them to be heard by the organizations and governments which make decisions that affect their lives. The number of people living in poverty in the UK has grown rapidly over the last 20 years, so Oxfam now works with groups in the UK as well as overseas.

The people Oxfam works with do all sorts of things. Some things are practical, and make a difference straight away; here are some examples: digging new wells (left), building *latrines*, making *compost* to improve the soil and grow better crops, and building stronger houses (below).

400 million people in the world live under military rule.

Long term benefits come from starting up a school to teach new skills for a living, and how to stay healthy.

Benefits also come from planting trees to improve the environment.

OXFAM INTERNATIONAL

Today there are organizations called Oxfam in 10 countries around the world. Each Oxfam is a separate organization, but they all share a similar way of working. They all help poor communities by funding small projects run by local people. Together these Oxfam **charities** are called 'Oxfam International'.

Our governments and *multinational companies* make decisions that affect us all wherever we live in the world. We can all help to change things if we work together like these women in Bangladesh and *campaign* to make the world a fairer place.

As many as 11 million people in the world are homeless.

HELPING PEOPLE TO HELP THEMSELVES

Oxfam does very little itself! Instead it raises money to help millions of people around the world do things for themselves. These people, like Rosie Ngabuzi and her women's group on the opposite page, have had enough of being poor and want to change things for the better.

RAISING MONEY

Oxfam raises money through its shops; from the mail-order catalogue which sells fair trade crafts and foods and stationery; through the Wastesaver **recycling** centre; from the UK government and the European Community, and from the United Nations. But ordinary people give Oxfam more money than each of these.

WAYS OF HELPING

Sometimes Oxfam helps by sending money to community groups and organizations; it organizes training to help people learn new skills; or sets up workshops so that people can get together to talk about their problems and find solutions. It also gives advice, encourages use of local radio and puts groups in different countries in touch so that they can learn from each other.

EMERGENCY HELP

Oxfam also helps people to survive in emergencies, by supplying materials to make shelters, blankets, clean water and sanitation.

 Local radio helps to keep people in touch with community projects.

8

Oxfam works in more than 70 countries.

Rosie Ngabuzi and her friends, in Tanzania, are changing things in their village. 'Our main problem was grinding maize. The nearest mill was several kilometres away,' she says. The women's group asked Oxfam for a loan to buy a grinding mill. Now everyone gets their maize ground in the village.

There have been other changes, too. 'After the mill arrived,' says Rosie, 'the village council recognized us as a strong group which could help to make the village a better place to live. Now some of the group are on the council, and one of us runs the committee that is in charge of the water-pump.'

More than one billion people don't have clean water or sanitation.

MEET EMMANUEL
KALLONGA IN TANZANIA

My name is Emmanuel Kallonga, and I'm in charge of Oxfam's work in Tanzania.

Oxfam began working here in 1976. We work with partners – local organizations and groups who know the area, the people, and the problems they face. Oxfam supports them by giving money, or by organizing training, or by finding specialist help or information. We also have staff who deal with emergencies – for example, working in the camps for **refugees** from Zaire, Burundi and Rwanda.

8.00am I start the day by going through yesterday's mail and faxes. Some will have come from Oxford, some from the other Oxfam offices in Tanzania, and some from the groups we support. I sort it all out into work that needs my attention, and work that I can pass to colleagues to deal with.

9.00am There's a letter from Ole Toroge, from an organization of Masai people in Loliondo. We have promised to pay their legal costs in a court. case about their land, and he wants to know how and when he will receive the money.

10.00am Mrs Bernadette Kinabo, the Director of Arumeru District Council, has come to see me. We are helping the council with a project to improve community water supplies, and she has come to tell me what has been happening since my visit last year.

Susan (one of our staff) and I discuss her new training session for women's groups.

By the year 2005, half the world's people will live in towns or cities.

> Some of our work is with children and young people with disabilities. We are providing rooms and equipment for special classes, and training teachers to work with children until they can join ordinary classes.

Sometimes I meet government officials to tell them about the communities we work with and the problems they face. In this way it is sometimes possible to influence government policies so that they don't ignore the poorest people.

2.00pm Every Monday, Roger, our Emergency co-ordinator, holds a meeting about the emergency programme for refugees sheltering in Tanzania. We talk about problems, and what's going well. On Tuesdays I run a meeting where we all discuss our work in Tanzania. Sometimes the meetings last for four hours! This afternoon Susan comes to talk to me about a training session she is setting up.

3.30 – 5pm During the day we receive telephone calls from Oxford, and from the other offices. They all need to talk to us – for an update about the situation of refugees, or about our colleagues' activities.

Oxfam cannot solve all Tanzania's problems. We see ourselves as part of a movement with the other organizations working to relieve poverty – all working together to find solutions.

> The staff working in the refugee camps call us every day using the radio link, so that we can keep in touch.

Every year, around 17 million people die from curable diseases.

MEET KAFIL AHMED
IN BANGLADESH

My job is to find organizations and groups who may need Oxfam's help.

I check that everything is going well, and help them solve their problems. Today I am going to visit Manab Mukti Sangstha (MMS), an organization working with some of the very poorest people in the country. These are people living on **chors**, low islands of silt built up in the rivers, which are easily flooded and washed away.

▼ **The approach to MMS.**

9.00am I leave Dhaka and travel by car and boat to MMS, where I am going to talk to the staff, and to visit one of the chor villages to see if the work done after last year's floods helped to save lives and belongings in this year's floods.

2.00pm I arrive at MMS's headquarters. They're helping people to be better prepared for the floods, so that they have some protection. I have been involved with MMS since they began working here — planning and suggesting how Oxfam could help — so I always enjoy visiting this project.

▲ **In this village, eight houses have already been washed away, and more are under threat. By next year there may not be a village here at all.**

▲ **Tagoria village, where the women are helping to build new homes above the flood levels.**

In Asia, 25 billion tonnes of soil are blown or washed away every year.

Sufia Khatun says: 'My husband is a labourer, and travels around to find work. My children go to the MMS school. MMS gave me a loan, and I bought two cows. I sell the milk they produce to support my family.'

2.15pm A meeting with all of the staff. They tell me how things have been going since my last visit. They are involved in a lot of projects: schools for children and classes for adults; health centres; lending money to help people to start small businesses or to buy seeds or animals; and training courses for people to learn new skills.

3.30pm I meet some of the women in Tagoria village. Last year, families here made earth platforms to build their homes above flood-level.

Although it was very hard work, they are very pleased that they did it. This year, none of the houses was flooded, and none of their animals was washed away.

7.00pm I go back to MMS's office, to meet the **accountants** and go through their books, to check that the money they receive from Oxfam is properly accounted for. It's been a long day, but I'm very happy with everything I've seen. I think this is a good use of Oxfam money.

Just like you, the children in Tagoria village have had to learn about how important it is to clean your teeth, to wash every day, and especially to wash your hands after using the *latrine*, and before eating. They showed me their hands – all clean!

13

80% of all illness in the world is caused by drinking dirty water.

MEET GELY
DE FRANÇA LIMA IN RECIFE, BRAZIL

I'm an **educator** with a project called Streets and Squares, which works with street children in Recife, Brazil. The streets and squares are where we meet the children. I've been doing this work for seven years, and I love it. I used to be a schoolteacher, and worked with children, but not children like this. People call them 'riff-raff'.

Most of the children are on the streets because of poverty. Many of the children do have families, but it's hard for their parents to find a job, and often the wages are too low to pay the rent and to buy food and clothes. They don't have the means to look after their children.

Some of the children don't have a home or family, or they have been thrown out because of glue-sniffing or stealing and the family can't cope with them any more. We try to find their families and we talk to the mothers. We might say: 'You, as a mother, have to take responsibility for this boy. He's your son, you can't just abandon him.'

9.00am This morning I'm arranging to get Edson a place on a computing course, in a project called A Helping Hand. He's very intelligent and keen to learn a skill that might get him a job.

11.00am I visit some of the children's families, to help them to understand and cope with their children, and to encourage them to see that their children attend school and get advice.

1.00pm Every afternoon, I go to the places where the children gather. At first, we just look at each other. The next day I go a bit closer. The day after, I ask their names, tell them my name and the name of the group, and ask if they would like to do a drawing or something. That's how I eventually win them over.

▲ **A lot of my work involves meeting the children's families and helping them to help their children.**

Nearly one in three people in the Third World cannot read or write.

Gely with Aparecida and Emanuel in Pistinha Square.

5.00pm Back to the office in Recife, which provides support for me and my co-workers and does fund-raising, **lobbying** and **publicity** work. I also meet some of the street children here.

10.00pm There are places where the children gather — squares, parks, at traffic lights, where they beg, and so on. Sometimes I work at night to check that the children I am working with are OK.

The work is exhausting, but it's great to see children trying to get back on their feet, giving up drugs, and building a new life.

Talking to the children at night, to make sure that they are all right.

In Brazil, 3 million 10 to 14-year-olds work growing tobacco, tea, sisal and sugar-cane on plantations.

MEET JADRANKA DAKIĆ
IN SERBIA

My name is Jadranka. I was born in Sarajevo 21 years ago. You have probably heard about Sarajevo; almost everyone must know there was a war there.

I am a **refugee**. I think the word refugee must sound sad in every language. It makes you think of homeless people, with no hope, with bags in their arms, who are not sure where they are going.

▲ **Jadranka and her Mum, Gorana, outside their home in the Collective Centre.**

▲ **Gorana in her vegetable garden. The gardens aren't big, but there is room to grow enough vegetables to have some for lunch every day.**

It was a very lonely journey from Sarajevo, even travelling with my mother and people I knew. We all had our own thoughts. People did not say it, but they knew they would never see their homes again.

My friends helped me to set up the library. We had to work hard to get it going, but now the children have a place to spend their free time, to read or listen to music. We still need more books for adults. ▶

16

Nearly 80% of refugees are women, children, and elderly people.

Milovan, a fellow refugee, in the carpentry workshop. We'll make doors, shelves, small cabinets – whatever we can sell. Oxfam has promised to help us with the materials.

I live in a refugee camp in Varna, a small village with two shops and a post office. We have been here for three years now. There are 200 of us in the camp, mostly from Bosnia and Herzegovina and Croatia. We all have different dialects and customs, and live together in a small area. We all have the same aim — just to survive. Almost every night we talk about the past, our homes, our schools, and our friends. Now these have gone and we can't have them back.

The local people don't like us very much — especially the older ones. The teenagers are better. Sometimes we go out with the local young people, but it saddens us when they talk about things we cannot afford.

Oxfam has helped us to rent a piece of land from a local farmer. The land has been divided into plots. We really don't know what we'd do without our gardens. It is probably the best thing Oxfam has done here; people have a lot of free time, but with the gardens they always have something to do.

I've become an English teacher. I have 10 students, and we have lessons twice a week. They want to learn English, because you can't do anything without knowing at least one 'world language'. I try to teach them everything I know. When they say: 'I understand, it is not complicated', I'm very proud.

I don't want to stay here, and I can't go back home. The only chance I have for a future is leaving the ex-Yugoslav territories. Anyway, I have hope. That is all I have.

For Milka and her daughter, Sladana, life is hard at the camp. Before the war, Sladana had all the medical care she needed.

About 10% of the world's population is disabled – more than 500 million people.

OXFAM'S WORK IN EMERGENCIES

In emergencies Oxfam works to keep people alive and healthy. We all need to be able to eat, sleep, drink and wash. When people are living crowded together in **refugee** camps, or suffering from shock or stress, disease can spread rapidly. Oxfam helps people survive.

Often, even before the newspaper and television reporters have realized that there is a disaster or emergency, Oxfam staff will be hard at work finding out what can be done.

Some emergencies are 'natural disasters', such as floods and earthquakes. Oxfam helps people to survive during the disaster, and to rebuild their homes and livelihoods afterwards.

Over the years, Oxfam engineers have developed systems to bring water to where it is needed, to purify it and to store it. Tap-stands enable people to use it.

There are more than 37 million refugees and displaced people in the world.

HOW CAN OXFAM HELP?

When Oxfam staff visit the emergency area, they talk to the people affected; they talk to any local organizations to find out what help is available locally; and then they work out whether Oxfam can help.

Often there are good local organizations, and all that they ask for from Oxfam is a specialist whose skills are not available locally; or maybe they need some plastic sheeting to make waterproof shelters, for example.

Often, when there is a disaster in a country where Oxfam has an office, staff will organize any help from Oxfam. When the disaster is very big and extra help is needed, specialist staff will be sent from Oxford. Sometimes, all the Oxfams put together a team.

A lot of Oxfam's work in emergencies takes place in Oxford – raising money, ordering equipment, filling in forms, organizing flights and so on. It may sound dull, but it is vital, as it makes everything else possible.

There are also 'man-made' disasters. Most of Oxfam's relief work is with people affected by conflict – with *displaced people* and refugees.

Oxfam has a store of emergency equipment – plastic sheeting, feeding kits, blankets, water equipment – ready to be sent anywhere in the world at a moment's notice.

2000 men, women, and children are killed or injured by land-mines every month.

OXFAM'S WORK IN SHOPS

Most people have seen or been in an Oxfam shop. There are about 830 of them in the UK – that's one in almost every shopping centre or high street. When TV or radio programmes mention a **charity** shop, it's nearly always an Oxfam shop. In fact, Oxfam opened the very first charity shop in the country in 1947.

VOLUNTEERS

Oxfam shops are run by volunteers, people of all ages who give some time as their way of helping Oxfam. Toral Shah helps out in the Kensington Oxfam shop. She says: 'I need to be doing something worthwhile. I wouldn't be here if I didn't believe in Oxfam's message.'

RECYCLED GOODS

'Oxfam shops are a way of **recycling** lots of things that people no longer need or want or have grown out of,' says Lucile Moon, another volunteer in Kensington. 'The shops sell second-hand clothes, glass, china, kitchen equipment and ornaments, shoes, books, records, tapes and CDs, hats, jewellery, toys, and games, pictures – you name it. And whatever you buy in an Oxfam shop, you are helping Oxfam's work.'

Oxfam shops can only work if people bring things for them to sell – a permanent bring-and-buy sale. You will often see posters in the window asking for particular things when they are running short – books, for example. You will also see posters telling you about special sales – maybe toys and games before Christmas.

These pictures show what happens when you take something into an Oxfam shop.

Simon is taking two jumpers to his local Oxfam shop.

In most countries, disabled people have less chance of getting a good education or a job.

Simon gives the jumpers to Toral, one of the volunteers.

Toral takes them upstairs to Gary. He checks them to see that they are good enough to sell. One is, so he puts a price ticket on it.

The good jumper goes on sale in the shop. The other jumper is worn out and not good enough to sell, so it's sent to Wastesaver, Oxfam's big recycling centre.

At Wastesaver, clothes are checked to see if they have buttons on. If they have, they are cut off and put into a bag to be sold. Then the jumper is packed into a bale, and resold to be made into rags for cleaning industrial machinery, or turned into carpet underlay. In this way, Wastesaver makes money for Oxfam.

Some of the shops sell Fair Trade crafts and food, as well. These are items made by groups overseas and bought specially to sell in the Oxfam shops. The people who made them have been paid a fair price for their work.

21

OXFAM'S WORK IN CAMPAIGNING

Oxfam has a network of volunteers who get involved in campaigns. They are ordinary people who want to make the world a better place to live. Here, a volunteer is asking supermarket customers if they would be prepared to pay higher prices to help producers.

'That's not fair!' is something we all say from time to time. Oxfam says it, too. That's why Oxfam **campaigns** to change the things in the world that are not fair, and can be put right.

Much of the food we eat is grown by people in **Third World** countries. Their crops are bought by **multinational companies** which make big profits. Let's look at what happens to coffee.

Coffee is one food crop grown by thousands of farmers in more than 40 countries.

Each farmer sells the coffee to international companies. When there is a poor harvest, there isn't enough to go round, so the companies bid against each other, and the price goes up. But when there is a good harvest, the price is low. Sometimes the farmers are paid less than it costs to grow the coffee. But whatever happens, the companies make sure they make a healthy profit. Farmers have no control over the prices paid for their crops. Many of them are too poor to buy enough food for their families.

Nearly 800 million people worldwide do not get enough food.

FAIR TRADE

Oxfam is campaigning to get companies to pay fair prices to the farmers and other producers. They are also persuading supermarkets that customers like the idea of producers being paid a fair price. The first Fair Trade produce was Cafédirect coffee – you may have seen it in the shops.

Cafédirect buys coffee grown by farmers in Nicaragua, Peru, Costa Rica, and Mexico. Some farmers in these countries have formed **co-operatives**, which makes them stronger and able to negotiate the price they are paid. The co-operatives sell to Cafédirect, because it pays more than the **market price**, so that the farmers earn more.

Picking ripe coffee beans.

Women sorting the beans, to throw out the bad ones.

'Before we started selling to Cafédirect, most of us could not afford medical treatment. The higher price we get means that now our co-operative can afford to pay a doctor who treats our families. I can afford more food for my family, and I can buy pens and school books for my children.'

23

190 million 10 to 14-year-olds in the Third World have to work.

OXFAM'S WORK IN COMMUNICATIONS

There are thousands of charities in the UK, all trying to raise money for their work. Oxfam is one of them. Before you can raise money, you have to tell people who you are, what you do, and how you do it. Once they know all these things about you, you have to keep reminding them that you are there, and that you still need their help.

UNDERSTANDING THE WORLD

Although raising money is important, Oxfam also needs to inform people. Oxfam believes that we should all know about the world we live in, and about the unfairness many families face in their lives. Then we can join others to make the world a better place.

▼ **Oxfam makes videos to show examples of projects overseas, or to fit in with particular *campaigns* or emergencies. Sometimes they are video news releases – pieces of film with information – which are sent to TV newsrooms to encourage them to include an item on the TV news.**

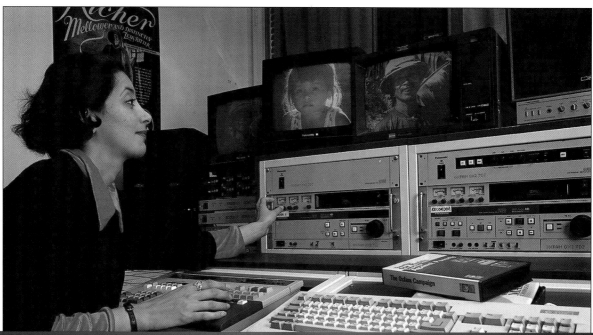

130 million children do not go to school.

Sometimes Oxfam asks celebrities to help to tell the public about Oxfam's work. Dawn French helped to explain what was happening in Rwanda.

There are lots of ways of telling people about Oxfam.

You may find an envelope dropping through your letter-box at home, or a leaflet falling out of a newspaper or magazine. This is a good way of getting information to hundreds of thousands of people. Some people read the letter or leaflet and send money, while others write to ask for more information about how they can help.

Adverts in the newspapers are a way of reminding people about Oxfam's work. Adverts are also used when there's a disaster and a lot of money is needed very quickly. Sometimes, when the emergency is very serious, there are appeals for money on TV.

Oxfam helps in schools in the UK, by publishing materials about people and the places they live in, and the problems they face.

Oxfam has staff in most of the countries it works in. They know the area and know what's going on, so they keep the rest of Oxfam in touch. The information they send is often sent to journalists and newspapers so that they can use it in articles and TV programmes.

Oxfam also produces books. Some of them are for students and journalists wanting to find detailed information. Others give practical information for the people Oxfam works with. You could read one to learn how to keep goats!

REBUILDING CAMBODIA

War, conflict, violence – it doesn't matter which word you use, there is an awful lot of it in the world today. Fighting which affects a few hundred people, or huge wars involving millions of people have the same results. Homes, towns and cities are destroyed. Wars split families, divide communities, and turn friends against each other. War makes people poor. It stops them going to work, so they can't earn money. It stops them farming, so they can't grow food. Wars injure and disable and kill people – mostly **civilians**.

More than 35,000 Cambodians have lost at least one limb by stepping on a land-mine as they have walked, or worked, or played. Twice that number have been killed.

HELPING THE VICTIMS

Every year, more and more of the money Oxfam spends on emergencies is spent helping people whose lives have been destroyed by war – helping them to survive, often in a strange country, with only the few belongings they could carry with them when they fled. And then Oxfam helps them to rebuild their homes and their livelihoods when they have returned home. For the victims, this can be when the really hard work and the danger begins.

Oxfam has been working in Cambodia for nearly 20 years, helping people to recover from **civil war**. By 1979 much of the country had been destroyed – roads, bridges, railways, hospitals, schools, factories, water pipelines and reservoirs. The Cambodian people faced a huge task – one that isn't finished yet.

In 1994, 4.7 million people were killed in conflicts around the world.

Oxfam has been helping by drilling wells and repairing water supplies; supplying tools and seeds and fertilizers; training people and reopening factories.

In 25 years of fighting, millions of **land-mines** were laid. Cambodia is one of the most heavily mined countries in the world, and has the greatest number of **amputees**. Mines are hard to spot. You don't know one is there until you tread on it. Just imagine going out with your friends, walking along, hearing a big explosion and then waking up – but without a foot or a hand. Mined fields cannot be planted with crops. Mined buildings cannot be lived in.

STARTING AGAIN

'Conditions were much better in the camp than they are here, but at least here we are in our own country, making our own lives. We have nothing here but our name. Even so, we prefer being here,' says Chuntahon, who has come home from a **refugee** camp in Thailand.

Clearing mines is a highly skilled and dangerous job needing nerves of steel.

Life was hard for families coming back to their villages after years in refugee camps. Oxfam helped families to set up new homes. Land must be cleared and crops planted, businesses started again, fish-ponds cleared and stocked, boats and fishing nets and lines bought. Women supporting families on their own still need a lot of help from their neighbours. Now people are learning how to trust each other and how to work together again.

With so many mines in Cambodia, it is vital that children and adults are taught what to look for, and what to do when they find one.

27

VISION FOR THE FUTURE

Oxfam's vision is a world without poverty, a world where everyone can meet their basic needs, and exercise their basic rights. This is a vision based on the dreams of the millions of people who shape the work that Oxfam does. Here are some of their dreams:

'We hope that peace will come and we can return to normal life. Living under war is bad. You can stand hunger and thirst, but losing people you cannot stand.'

'My dream is that I will be able to buy a cup of rice or a little milk to feed my child.'

'I want my children to be educated. Knowledge will help them to survive, to participate in life, to make their contribution.'

'I would like there to be good services in my village, and a health-post so that we can keep healthy.'

'For the future, I hope we'll get our plots of land and be able to build our houses and to live in peace.'

'We hope for a well to give us good water all year round, because our children get sick from drinking dirty water.'

'I hope that the group will grow in confidence, and that we can begin to change attitudes towards disabled people.'

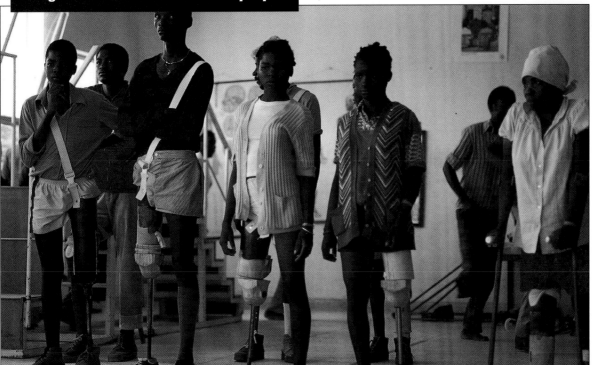

FURTHER INFORMATION

FOR YOU

Did you know that you can find Oxfam on the internet? Look for One world On-line: (http://www.oneworld.org/oxfam/), where you can find lots more information and material about the countries Oxfam works in, and about the people Oxfam works with and Oxfam **campaigns**.

If your class is doing a project, you could write to the Supporters' Information Team and ask for information. They have a range of free materials for young people. If you write to them, please write just one letter, and they will send you an information sheet for you to photocopy.

Materials specially written for you include information about Bangladesh, Brazil, the Caribbean, Egypt, India and Kenya. There is also a new series of leaflets: *Understanding Oxfam; Food* – about diet, hunger, famine, and harvest; *Basic rights – shelter, food, water; Conflict; Environment*.

Write to: Supporters' Information, Oxfam, 274 Banbury Road, Oxford, OX2 7DZ.

Did you know that if you are 12-years-old or more, you can help in an Oxfam shop? Well you can! Why don't you call in at your local shop and ask how you could help.

FOR YOUR TEACHER

Oxfam Supporters' Information Team answers many enquiries a year, many of them from young people and teachers. As well as the information sheets listed above, free materials include:

Resources for Schools and Youth Groups, a catalogue of materials about the causes and effects of global poverty. Produced by Oxfam and other agencies, the materials offer practical and imaginative ways to help explore these issues.

Oxfam: Annual Review Summary, Understanding Oxfam (for primary or secondary schools), a Brief History of Oxfam, International Oxfams, Organisation of Oxfam, Shops, Recycling, What your donation could do, Fundraising ideas.

Countries: the Andes, Bangladesh, Brazil, Cambodia, Eastern Europe, Eritrea, Ethiopia, India, Indonesia, Mozambique, Senegal, South Africa, Sudan, Vietnam.

Topics: Anti-personnel mines, Debt, Education and Training, Fair Trade, Health, Hunger and Famine, Recycling, Refugees, Street Children, Technology, Water, Women.

New materials are being produced all the time. The unit cannot supply free photographs or posters.

For more information, please phone Supporters' Information on 01865 313600, or write to them at the address above. Or e-mail: Oxfam @oxfam.org.uk. Or you could find out more about Oxfam's materials for schools on Heinemann World (http://www.heinemann.co.uk), an educational site for teachers, students, and librarians, and you can also use the internet address above to find out more about Oxfam.

There are also three Oxfam Resource Centres, which can offer help from specialist education staff, inservice training, curriculum support and advice. For more information and the addresses, phone: Cardiff (01222 757 067), Glasgow (0141 331 2725) or London (0171 249 2632).

GLOSSARY

accountants people who keep records (books) about an individual's or a group's money

amputee someone who has had to have an arm or a leg cut off (amputated)

bustees areas of cities in Bangladesh where the poorest people live. They are usually overcrowded, and have no electricity or water or sanitation.

campaign an activity that is designed to tell people about something, or to get something changed

charity a non-profit-making organization set up to help those in need

chors areas of low, flat land or islands, formed by silt which has been left there by slow-moving rivers

civilians people who are not in the armed forces

civil war a war between groups of people living in the same country

compost a preparation of rotted animal and plant matter, dug into the soil to make it richer

co-operative a group of people who work together and share their profits

displaced people people who leave their homes because of war or disaster, or because they are bullied or threatened, and who move to another part of their own country

educator someone who teaches

land-mine a buried bomb which explodes when you step on it

latrines simple toilets

lobbying meeting or writing to people who can make changes in local council or national government policies

market price the price people or companies will pay

military rule government of a country by the armed forces, with no free elections

multinational companies companies which have business interests in different countries around the world

publicity information that makes something known; advertising

recycling re-using something; making something new out of something old; using scrap to make other things, such as sandals out of car tyres

refugees displaced people who move to another country

Third World the poorer countries of Asia, Africa and Latin America that are gradually developing better economic and social conditions

INDEX